The WORLD'S Greatest
Collection of
QUOTES FOR *Moms*

The WORLD'S Greatest Collection of QUOTES FOR *Moms*

BARBOUR
PUBLISHING

Contents

The Circle of Love

And now these three remain:
faith, hope and love. But the
greatest of these is love.

1 CORINTHIANS 13:13 NIV

It is not a slight thing when they,
who are so fresh from God, love us.

CHARLES DICKENS

There is only one pretty child
in the world, and every mother has it.

CHINESE PROVERB

Where we love is home—
home that our feet may leave,
but not our hearts.

OLIVER WENDELL HOLMES SR.

*Mother's love is peace. It need
not be acquired; it need not be deserved.*

ERICH FROMM

*A mother's heart and a mother's faith
And a mother's steadfast love
Were fashioned by the angels
And sent from God above.*

UNKNOWN

*By the grace of God I am what I am:
and his grace which was bestowed
upon me was not in vain; but I
laboured more abundantly than they
all: yet not I, but the grace of God
which was with me.*

1 CORINTHIANS 15:10 KJV

*The heart of a mother is a deep abyss
at the bottom of which you will
always find forgiveness.*

HONORÉ DE BALZAC

A mother's arms are made of
tenderness, and children sleep
soundly in them.

VICTOR HUGO

God pardons like a mother, who kisses
the offense into everlasting forgiveness.

HENRY WARD BEECHER

A mother's love is like a stream
That flows forever to the sea.
It never ends, because God sends
Replenishment abundantly.
Love's a strange commodity—
The more you give, the more you get.
Though you may try to drain it dry,
It's never been accomplished yet.

JANICE LEWIS CLARK

God loves us the way a good mother loves—totally, unconditionally, with a nurturing and ever-present care. In fact, as mothers, our love for our children is only a dim reflection of the love God has for His people.

ELLYN SANNA

Love never gives up, never loses faith, is always hopeful, and endures through every circumstance.

1 CORINTHIANS 13:7 NLT

A mother's love!—how sweet the name!
The holiest, purest, tenderest flame
That kindles from above;
Within a heart of earthly mold
As much of heaven as heart can hold
Nor through eternity grows cold—
That is a mother's love.

MONTGOMERY

Maternal love: a miraculous substance which God multiplies as He divides it.

VICTOR HUGO

A mother's love is indeed the golden link
that binds youth to age; and he is still but
a child, however time may have furrowed
his cheek, or silvered his brow, who can
yet recall, with a softened heart, the fond
devotion, or the gentle chidings of the
best friend that God ever gave us.

CHRISTIAN NESTELL BOVEE

The mother love is like God's love;
He loves us not because we are lovable,
but because it is His nature to love,
and because we are His children.

EARL RINEY

Why did God make mothers?
To teach us how to love Him.
To teach us how to love.

LARISSA CARRICK

*Chosen by God for this new life of love,
dress in the wardrobe God picked
out for you: compassion, kindness,
humility, quiet strength, discipline.*

COLOSSIANS 3:12 MSG

*Motherhood: All love
begins and ends there.*

ROBERT BROWNING

*Maternal love!
Thou word that sums all bliss.*

POLLOCK

*It is often said that patience is a virtue. It's
also a reflection of a mother's love. To be patient
and long-suffering with one's family is the true
measure of love. A mother's patience is a fine
example to her children.*

WANDA E. BRUNSTETTER

Mother love is the fuel that enables a normal human being to do the impossible.

UNKNOWN

Mother is the bank where we deposit all our hurts and worries.

UNKNOWN

A mother's love for her child is like nothing else in the world. It knows no law, no pity; it dares all things and crushes down remorselessly all that stands in its path.

AGATHA CHRISTIE

Holy as heaven a mother's tender love, the love of many prayers and many tears which changes not with dim, declining years.

CAROLINE NORTON

Some are kissing mothers, and some are scolding mothers, but it is love just the same, and most mothers kiss and scold together.

PEARL S. BUCK

A man loves his sweetheart the most, his wife the best, but his mother the longest.

IRISH PROVERB

Mothers reflect God's loving presence on earth.

WILLIAM R. WEBB

There is no friendship, no love, like that of the parent for the child.

HENRY WARD BEECHER

Being a full-time mother is one of the highest salaried jobs. . .since the payment is pure love.

MILDRED B. VERMONT

A father may turn his back on his child, brothers and sisters may become inveterate enemies, husbands may desert their wives, wives their husbands. But a mother's love endures through all.

WASHINGTON IRVING

*One lamp—thy mother's love—amid the stars
Shall lift its pure flame changeless, and before
The throne of God, burn through eternity—
Holy—as it was lit and lent thee here.*

NATHANIEL PARKER WILLIS

*We never know the love of our parents
for us till we have become parents.*

HENRY WARD BEECHER

*Children need love, especially
when they do not deserve it.*

HAROLD HULBERT

*Mothers hold their children's hands
for a short while, but their hearts forever.*

UNKNOWN

*I never knew how much love
my heart could hold until
someone called me "Mommy."*

UNKNOWN

*A mother's love perceives
no impossibilities.*

PADDOCK

*No gift to your mother can
ever equal her gift to you—life.*

ANONYMOUS

Expecting—and Experiencing

*One of the oldest human needs is having
someone to wonder where you are
when you don't come home at night.*

MARGARET MEAD

*The most important piece of
clothing you must wear is love.
Love is what binds us all
together in perfect harmony.*

COLOSSIANS 3:14 NLT

*Who takes the child by the
hand takes the mother by the heart.*

GERMAN PROVERB

*If nature had arranged that husbands and wives
should have children alternately, there would
never be more than three in a family.*

LAWRENCE HOUSMAN

Encourage those who are timid.
Take tender care of those who are weak.
Be patient with everyone.

1 Thessalonians 5:14 nlt

A babe in a house is a wellspring of pleasure.

Martin Tupper

A baby is a bit of stardust
fallen from the hand of God.

Unknown

When the first baby laughed for the first time,
the laugh broke into a thousand pieces and
they all went skipping about, and that was the
beginning of the fairies.

James M. Barrie

Dear Lord, thank You so much for my baby's smiles. Her laughter fills me with joy. She is so precious to me, God. I don't have enough words to express my love and gratitude. All I can say is thank You.

A glad heart makes a happy face.
PROVERBS 15:13 NLT

Hush, my dear, lie still and slumber,
Holy angels guard thy bed!
Heavenly blessings without number
Gently falling on thy head.
ISAAC WATTS

A baby is an inestimable
blessing and a bother.
MARK TWAIN

*I actually remember feeling delight,
at two o'clock in the morning, when
the baby woke for his feed, because I
so longed to have another look at him.*

MARGARET DRABBLE

*Babies are always more trouble than
you thought—and more wonderful.*

CHARLES OSGOOD

*Give all your worries and cares to God, for he
cares about what happens to you.*

1 PETER 5:7 NLT

*I begin to love this little creature, and to
anticipate his birth as a fresh twist to a knot,
which I do not wish to untie.*

MARY WOLLSTONECRAFT

Think always that, having the child at your breast and having it in your arms, you have God's blessing there.

ELIZABETH CLINTON

O young thing, your mother's lovely armful! How sweet the fragrance of your body!

EURIPIDES

Making the decision to have a child—it's momentous. It is to decide forever to have your heart go walking around outside your body.

ELIZABETH STONE

He will love you and bless you and increase your numbers. He will bless the fruit of your womb.

DEUTERONOMY 7:13 NIV

The moment a child is born, the mother is also born. She never existed before. The woman existed, but the mother, never. A mother is something absolutely new.

RAJNEESH

A baby will make love stronger, days shorter, nights longer, bankrolls smaller, homes happier, clothes shabbier, the past forgotten, and the future worth living for.

ANONYMOUS

We witness a miracle every time a child enters into life. But those who make their journey home across time and miles, growing within the hearts of those who wait to love them, are carried on the wings of destiny and placed among us by God's very own hands.

KRISTI LARSON

*Who is getting more pleasure
from this rocking, the baby or me?*
NANCY THAYER

*When a woman gives birth, she has a hard time,
there's no getting around it. But when the baby
is born, there is joy in the birth. This new life in
the world wipes out memory of the pain.*
JOHN 16:21 MSG

*A baby is God's opinion
that the world should go on.*
CARL SANDBURG

*A baby is. . .a rose with all its
sweetest leaves yet folded.*
LORD BYRON

*A baby is something you
carry inside you for nine months,
in your arms for three years, and
in your heart till the day you die.*
MARY MASON

*A mother's joy begins when new life is
stirring inside. . .
when a tiny heartbeat is heard for the
very first time,
and a playful kick reminds her that she
is never alone.*
UNKNOWN

Mothers and
Children

All your sons will be taught by the LORD,
and great will be your children's peace.

ISAIAH 54:13 NIV

A child is the root of the heart.

CAROLINA MARIA DE JESUS

The soul is healed
by being with children.

FYODOR DOSTOEVSKY

Nothing is so beautiful as a mother with her
children gathered around her.

UNKNOWN

Mother is the name for God in the lips and
hearts of little children.

WILLIAM MAKEPEACE THACKERAY

A rich child often sits in a poor mother's lap.

<small>DANISH PROVERB</small>

As one whom his mother comforteth,
so will I comfort you.

<small>ISAIAH 66:13 KJV</small>

She never quite leaves her children
at home, even when she doesn't
take them along.

<small>MARGARET CULKIN BANNING</small>

Children are a lot like wet cement.
Whatever falls on them makes an impression.

<small>HAIM GINOTT</small>

Every child comes with the message that
God is not yet discouraged of man.

<small>RABINDRANATH TAGORE</small>

*Your children are always your
"babies," even if they have gray hair.*
JANET LEIGH

*Children are the living messages
we send to a time we will not see.*
JOHN W. WHITEHEAD

*Children are a gift from the LORD;
they are a reward from him.*
PSALM 127:3 NLT

*In the eyes of its mother
every beetle is a gazelle.*
AFRICAN PROVERB

*No joy in nature is so sublimely affecting as the
joy of a mother at the good fortune of her child.*
JEAN PAUL RICHTER

*The future destiny of a child is
always the work of its mother.*
NAPOLEON

*Nothing you do for children is ever wasted. They
seem not to notice us, hovering, averting our
eyes, and they seldom offer thanks, but what we
do for them is never wasted.*
GARRISON KEILLOR

*Point your kids in the right direction—
when they're old they won't be lost.*
PROVERBS 22:6 MSG

*If we are to have real peace,
we must begin with the children.*
MAHATMA GANDHI

To be in your children's memories tomorrow,
you have to be in their lives today.

ANONYMOUS

When I approach a child, he inspires in me
two sentiments; tenderness for what he is,
and respect for what he may become.

LOUIS PASTEUR

Each day of our lives we make deposits
in the memory banks of our children.

CHARLES R. SWINDOLL

Her children arise up, and call
her blessed; her husband also,
and he praiseth her.

PROVERBS 31:28 KJV

A young boy said to his mother, "How old were you when I was born?" His mother replied, "Twenty-three." "Wow," he said, "that's a lot of time we missed spending together."

UNKNOWN

Children are the anchors
that hold a mother to life.

SOPHOCLES

*To a child's ear, "mother"
is magic in any language.*

ARLENE BENEDICT

You know children are growing up when they start asking questions that have answers.

JOHN J. PLOMP

Children seldom misquote you.
In fact, they usually repeat word for word what
you shouldn't have said.

UNKNOWN

I prayed for this child, and GOD gave
me what I asked for. And now I have
dedicated him to GOD.

1 SAMUEL 1:27–28 MSG

It is easier to build strong children
than to repair broken men.

FREDERICK DOUGLASS

A mother's children are portraits of herself.

UNKNOWN

You know your children are growing up when they stop asking you where they came from and refuse to tell you where they're going.

P. J. O'ROURKE

Discipline your son, and he will give you peace; he will bring delight to your soul.

PROVERBS 29:17 NIV

Never fear spoiling children by making them too happy. Happiness is the atmosphere in which all good affections grow.

THOMAS BRAY

We are apt to forget that children watch examples better than they listen to preaching.

ROY L. SMITH

A hundred years from now, it will
not matter what my bank account was,
the sort of house I lived in, or the make
of car I drove. But the world may be
different, because I was important
in the life of a child.

UNKNOWN

If you plan for one year, plant rice.
If you plan for ten years, plant a tree.
If you plan for one hundred
years, educate a child.

CHINESE PROVERB

The Family Bond

He blesses the home of the righteous.

PROVERBS 3:33 NIV

The love of a family is life's greatest blessing.

ANONYMOUS

Mothers of daughters are daughters of mothers and have remained so, in circles joined to circles, since time began.

SIGNE HAMMER

The art of mothering is handed down from one generation to the next.

WENDY JEAN RUHL

What do girls do who haven't any mothers to help them through their troubles?

LOUISA MAY ALCOTT

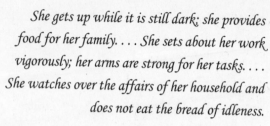

She gets up while it is still dark; she provides
food for her family. . . . She sets about her work
vigorously; her arms are strong for her tasks. . . .
She watches over the affairs of her household and
does not eat the bread of idleness.

PROVERBS 31:15, 17, 27 NIV

When a mother exudes a sense of peace and
tranquility, her family feels calm. Peacefulness
brings healing to a troubled spirit. A peaceful
mother is like a medicinal balm. Peace and
assurance of Mother's love are necessary
ingredients for a happy home.

Use your worldly resources to benefit others and
make friends. In this way, your generosity stores
up a reward for you in heaven.

LUKE 16:9 NLT

The thing about mothers is. . .
All their children are geniuses.

The thing about mothers is. . .
They are each and every one
the best cook in the entire world.

The thing about mothers is. . .
They always take your side in an argument—
unless you're arguing with them.

The thing about mothers is. . .
No matter how old you get, they're the best
people to have around when you're sick.

The thing about mothers is. . .
You can't lie when you're
looking into their eyes.

The thing about mothers is. . .
When they're on a diet, everyone in the family
has to be on a diet, too.

Mother's soft touch and gentle words of love,
Are like healing balm from heaven above.

WANDA E. BRUNSTETTER

Happy the home when God is there,
And love fills every breast;
When one their wish,
and one their prayer,
And one their heavenly rest.
Happy the home where Jesus' name
Is sweet to every ear;
Where children early speak His fame,
And parents hold Him dear.

HENRY WARE JR.

It is not our exalted feelings, it is our
sentiments that build the necessary home.

ELIZABETH BOWEN

A daughter is a mother's gender partner,
her closest ally in the family confederacy,
an extension of her self. And mothers are
their daughters' role model, their biological
and emotional road map, the arbiter of
all their relationships.

VICTORIA SECUNDA

The LORD is my strength, my shield
from every danger. I trust in him
with all my heart. He helps me,
and my heart is filled with joy.
I burst out in songs of thanksgiving.

PSALM 28:7 NLT

A man's work is from sun to sun,
but a mother's work is never done.

UNKNOWN

The family is a haven in a heartless world.

CHRISTOPHER LASCH

*Families are like fudge. . .mostly
sweet with a few nuts.*

UNKNOWN

*A family is a unit composed not only of
children but of men, women, an occasional
animal, and the common cold.*

OGDEN NASH

*LORD, you have assigned me my
portion and my cup; you have made
my lot secure. The boundary lines have
fallen for me in pleasant places; surely
I have a delightful inheritance.*

PSALM 16:5–6 NIV

*An ounce of blood is worth
more than a pound of friendship.*

SPANISH PROVERB

You don't choose your family. They are God's gift to you, as you are to them.

DESMOND TUTU

To us, family means putting your arms around each other and being there.

BARBARA BUSH

The LORD says, "I will guide you along the best pathway for your life. I will advise you and watch over you."

PSALM 32:8 NLT

Call it a clan, call it a network, call it a tribe, call it a family. Whatever you call it, whoever you are, you need one.

JANE HOWARD

In time of test, family is best.

BURMESE PROVERB

The only rock I know that stays steady, the only institution I know that works is the family.

LEE IACOCCA

What greater thing is there for human souls than to feel that they are joined for life—to be with each other in silent unspeakable memories.

GEORGE ELIOT

May your father and mother be glad; may she who gave you birth rejoice!

PROVERBS 23:25 NIV

Whatever they grow up to be, they are still our
children, and the one most important of all the
things we can give to them is unconditional
love. Not a love that depends on anything at all
except that they are our children.

ROSALEEN DICKSON

The love of a family is life's greatest blessing.
The house does not rest upon the ground, but
upon a woman.

MEXICAN PROVERB

*A happy family is
but an earlier heaven.*
GEORGE BERNARD SHAW

The LORD shall increase you more and more, you
and your children. Ye are blessed of the LORD
which made heaven and earth.

PSALM 115:14–15 KJV

*Treat your family like friends
and your friends like family.*

*What the child says,
he has heard at home.*

AFRICAN PROVERB

*There are times when parenthood seems nothing
but feeding the mouth that bites you.*

PETER DE VRIES

*Tribute to
Mom*

When she speaks, her words are wise, and kindness is the rule when she gives instructions.

PROVERBS 31:26 NLT

I remember my mother's prayers, and they have always followed me. They have clung to me all my life.

ABRAHAM LINCOLN

A mother is the truest friend we have, when trials, heavy and sudden, fall upon us; when adversity takes the place of prosperity; when friends who rejoice with us in our sunshine desert us; when troubles thicken around us; still will she cling to us, and endeavor by her kind precepts and counsels to dissipate the clouds of darkness, and cause peace to return to our hearts.

WASHINGTON IRVING

All I am, I owe to my mother. I attribute all my success in life to the moral, intellectual, and physical education I received from her.

GEORGE WASHINGTON

Who ran to help me when I fell,
And would some pretty story tell,
Or kiss the place to make it well?
My mother.

JANE AND ANN TAYLOR

There never was a woman like her. She was gentle as a dove and brave as a lioness. . . . The memory of my mother and her teachings were, after all, the only capital I had to start life with, and on that capital I have made my way.

ANDREW JACKSON

You should be known for the beauty that comes from within, the unfading beauty of a gentle and quiet spirit, which is so precious to God.

1 PETER 3:4 NLT

Because I feel that,
in the heavens above,
The angels, whispering to one another
Can find, among their burning
terms of love,
None so devotional as
that of "Mother."
Therefore by that dear name I
have long called you,
You who are more than mother to me.

EDGAR ALLAN POE

Moms

Wife, companion, sweetheart, friend,
One on whom we all depend,
Chauffer, laundress, cook, and baker,
Casserole and cookie maker,
Seamstress, skilled in many arts,
Mending clothes and broken hearts,
Girl Scout leader, Sunday school teacher,
Confidante, advisor, preacher,
Bargain hunter, tutor, nurse,
Keeper of the family purse,
Neighbor, cousin, daughter, niece,
Making beds and making peace,
Always smiling, always giving,
What a busy life they're living,
Feeding children, dogs, and cats,
How do they wear so many hats?

JANICE LEWIS CLARK

A mother is not a person to lean on, but a person
to make leaning unnecessary.

DOROTHY CANFIELD FISHER

The successful mother, the mother who does her part in rearing and training aright the boys and girls who are to be the men and women of the next generation, is of greater use to the community. . . . She is more important by far than the successful statesman or businessman or artist or scientist.

THEODORE ROOSEVELT

My sainted mother taught me a devotion to God and a love to country which have ever sustained me in my many lonely and bitter moments of decision in distant and hostile lands. To her, I yield anew a son's reverent thanks.

GENERAL DOUGLAS MACARTHUR

We are God's workmanship, created in Christ Jesus to do good works, which God prepared in advance for us to do.

EPHESIANS 2:10 NIV

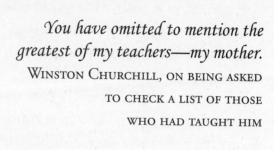

You have omitted to mention the greatest of my teachers—my mother.
WINSTON CHURCHILL, ON BEING ASKED TO CHECK A LIST OF THOSE WHO HAD TAUGHT HIM

Like kites without strings and butterfly wings, my mother taught me to soar with my dreams.
WILLIAM H. McMURRY III

There was a place in childhood that I remember well, And there a voice of sweetest tone bright fairy tales did tell.
SAMUEL LOVER, *MY MOTHER DEAR*

Mom—a simple little word that conjures up fond memories, warm feelings, and a sense of wonder at all she manages to accomplish.

Charm is deceptive, and beauty is fleeting; but a woman who fears the LORD is to be praised.

PROVERBS 31:30 NIV

When God thought of mother, He must have laughed with satisfaction, and framed it quickly—so rich, so deep, so divine, so full of soul, power, and beauty, was the conception.

HENRY WARD BEECHER

I think my life began with waking up and loving my mother's face.

GEORGE ELIOT

A mother is a person who seeing there are only four pieces of pie for five people, promptly announces she never did care for pie.

TENNEVA JORDAN

Women know
The way to rear up children (to be just)
They know a simple,
merry, tender knack
Of tying sashes, fitting baby shoes
And stringing pretty words
that make no sense.

ELIZABETH BARRETT BROWNING

Hundreds of dewdrops to greet the dawn,
Hundreds of bees in the purple clover,
Hundreds of butterflies on the lawn,
But only one mother the wide world over.

GEORGE COOPER

"There are many virtuous and capable women in the world, but you surpass them all!"

PROVERBS 31:29 NLT

Most of all the other beautiful things in life come by twos and threes, by dozens and hundreds. Plenty of roses, stars, sunsets, rainbows, brothers and sisters, aunts and cousins, comrades and friends—but only one mother in the whole world.

KATE DOUGLAS WIGGIN

My mother had a slender, small body, but a large heart—a heart so large that everybody's joys found welcome in it, and hospitable accommodation.

MARK TWAIN

No painter's brush, nor poet's pen
In justice to her fame
Has ever reached half high enough
To write a mother's name.

UNKNOWN

Be an example to all believers in what you teach,
in the way you live, in your love, your faith,
and your purity.

1 TIMOTHY 4:12 NLT

If I had a flower for each time I
thought of my mother, I could walk in
my garden forever.

UNKNOWN

There is no velvet so soft as a mother's
lap, no rose as lovely as her smile, no path so
flowery as that imprinted with her footsteps.

ARCHIBALD THOMPSON

Our mother is the sweetest and
Most delicate of all.
She knows more of paradise
Than angels can recall.
She's not only beautiful
But passionately young,
Playful as a kid, yet wise
As one who has lived long.
Her love is like the rush of life,
A bubbling, laughing spring
That runs through all like liquid light
And makes the mountains sing.

ANONYMOUS

First thing in the morning, she dresses for work,
rolls up her sleeves, eager to get started. She
senses the worth of her work, is in no hurry to
call it quits for the day.

PROVERBS 31:17–18 MSG

The mother is everything—she is our consolation in sorrow, our hope in misery, and our strength in weakness. She is the source of love, mercy, sympathy, and forgiveness. He who loses his mother loses a pure soul who blesses and guards him constantly.

KAHLIL GIBRAN

He blesses the home of the righteous.
PROVERBS 3:33 NIV

Nobody knows of the work it makes
To keep the home together.
Nobody knows of the steps it takes,
Nobody knows—but Mother.

ANONYMOUS

We only have one mom, one life. Don't wait for the tomorrows to tell Mom you love her.

UNKNOWN

*When I was a child, my mother said to
me, "If you become a soldier, you'll be a
general. If you become a monk, you'll
end up as the pope." Instead I became
a painter and wound up as Picasso.*

PABLO PICASSO

*You may have tangible wealth untold:
Caskets of jewels and coffers of gold.
Richer than I you can never be
I had a mother who read to me.*

STRICKLAND GILLILAN

The Lighter Side

*Be strong and steady, always enthusiastic
about the Lord's work, for you know that
nothing you do for the Lord is ever useless.*
1 CORINTHIANS 15:58 NLT

*You know you're a mom
when you say things like. . .
Don't ask me; ask your father.*

*You know you're a mom when
you say things like. . .
Were you raised in a barn?
Close the door!*

*You know you're a mom
when you say things like. . .
Get your elbows off the table.*

You know you're a mom
when you say things like. . .
Who said life was supposed to be fair?

You know you're a mom
when you say things like. . .
Because I said so. That's why.

You know you're a mom
when you say things like. . .
If I didn't love you so much, I wouldn't punish
you. I would let you do whatever you wanted.

You know you're a mom
when you say things like. . .
You're not leaving the house dressed like that!
What will other parents think?

*You know you're a mom
when you say things like. . .
Don't use that tone with me!*

*You know you're a mom
when you say things like. . .
Two wrongs don't make a right.*

*You know you're a mom
when you say things like. . .
Act your age.*

*You know you're a mom
when you say things like. . .
Wipe your feet!*

A good woman is hard to find,
and worth far more than diamonds.

PROVERBS 31:10 MSG

The best way to keep children
home is to make the home atmosphere
pleasant—and let the air
out of the tires.

DOROTHY PARKER

A suburban mother's role is to deliver children
obstetrically once, and by car forever after.

PETER DE VRIES

Sweater, n.: garment worn by child when its
mother is feeling chilly.

AMBROSE BIERCE

*If evolution really works, how come
mothers only have two hands?*

MILTON BERLE

*Be of good courage, and he shall
strengthen your heart, all ye that hope
in the LORD.*

PSALM 31:24 KJV

*It's not easy being a mother. If it were easy,
fathers would do it.*

*Sing out loud in the car even, or especially,
if it embarrasses your children.*

MARILYN PENLAND

*Insanity is hereditary; you
get it from your children.*

SAM LEVENSON

*The one thing children wear
out faster than shoes is parents.*

JOHN J. PLOMP

*[Jesus said,] "Come to me, all you who are weary
and burdened, and I will give you rest."*

MATTHEW 11:28 NIV

*My mother had a great deal of trouble with me,
but I think she enjoyed it.*

MARK TWAIN

*My mother's menu consisted of two choices:
take it or leave it.*
BUDDY HACKETT

*Any child can tell you that the sole
purpose of a middle name is so he can
tell when he's really in trouble.*
DENNIS FAKES

*Having a family is like having a bowling
alley installed in your brain.*
MARTIN MULL

*If your baby is beautiful and perfect,
never cries or fusses, sleeps on schedule
and burps on demand, an angel all
the time, you're the grandma.*
THERESA BLOOMINGDALE

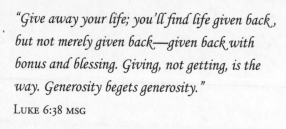

"Give away your life; you'll find life given back, but not merely given back—given back with bonus and blessing. Giving, not getting, is the way. Generosity begets generosity."
LUKE 6:38 MSG

*Think of stretch marks
as pregnancy service stripes.*
JOYCE ARMOR

*Even when freshly washed and
relieved of all obvious confections,
children tend to be sticky.*
FRAN LEBOWITZ

*You can learn many things from children.
How much patience you have, for instance.*
FRANKLIN P. JONES

The only thing that counts is faith
expressing itself through love.

GALATIANS 5:6 NIV

*People who say they sleep like
a baby usually don't have one.*

L. J. BURKE

The joys of motherhood are never
fully experienced until the
children are in bed.

UNKNOWN

For Further
Thought

Don't get tired of doing what is good. Don't get discouraged and give up, for we will reap a harvest of blessing at the appropriate time.

GALATIANS 6:9 NLT

God could not be everywhere, and therefore He made mothers.

RUDYARD KIPLING

There are only two lasting bequests we can hope to give our children. One is roots; the other, wings.

HODDING CARTER

[Your children] may forget what you said, but they will never forget how you made them feel.

CARL W. BUECHNER

A mother understands what a child does not say.

JEWISH PROVERB

The mother's heart is the child's schoolroom.

HENRY WARD BEECHER

I know whom I have believed, and am persuaded that he is able to keep that which I have committed unto him against that day.

2 TIMOTHY 1:12 KJV

A mother is she who can take the place of all others but whose place no one else can take.

CARDINAL MERMILLOD

The first and best school of politeness, as of character, is always the home, where woman is the teacher. The manners of society at large are but the reflexes of the manners of our collective homes, neither better nor worse.

J. L. NICHOLS

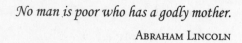

No man is poor who has a godly mother.

ABRAHAM LINCOLN

*Commit to the LORD whatever you do,
and your plans will succeed.*

PROVERBS 16:3 NIV

*There is no influence so
powerful as that of the mother.*

SARAH JOSEPHA HALE

*Our goal is to steadily turn our children
away from their earthly parents, who
will let them down, toward a heavenly Father
who will always be there for them and in
whose arms they will always be secure.*

SUSAN ALEXANDER YATES

Pride is one of the seven deadly sins;
but it cannot be the pride of a mother in her
children, for that is compound of two cardinal
virtues—faith and hope.
CHARLES DICKENS

You train a child until age ten.
After that, you only influence them.
UNKNOWN

The great academy, a mother's knee.
THOMAS CARLYLE

The joy of the LORD is your strength.
NEHEMIAH 8:10 KJV

There is only one way to bring
up a child in the way that he should go
and that is to travel that way yourself.
ABRAHAM LINCOLN

Children miss nothing in sizing up their parents.
If you are only half convinced of your beliefs,
they will quickly discern that fact.

JAMES DOBSON

Training a child to follow Christ is easy for
parents; all they have to do is lead the way.

UNKNOWN

The best inheritance a [mother] can
give [her] children is a few minutes of
[her] time each day.

O. A. BATTISTA

People are what their mothers make them.

RALPH WALDO EMERSON

And all thy children shall be taught of the LORD;
and great shall be the peace of thy children.

ISAIAH 54:13 KJV

If you can give your son or daughter only one gift, let it be enthusiasm.

BRUCE BARTON

The work will wait while you show your child the rainbow, but the rainbow won't wait while you do the work.

PATRICIA CLAFFORD

The conscience of children is formed by the influences that surround them; their notions of good and evil are the result of the moral atmosphere they breathe.

JEAN PAUL RICHTER

When you lead your sons and daughters in the good way, let your words be tender and caressing, in terms of discipline that wins the heart's assent.

ELIJAH BEN SOLOMON ZALMAN

The wise woman builds her house, but with her own hands the foolish one tears hers down.

PROVERBS 14:1 NIV

Every mother is like Moses. She does not enter the Promised Land. She prepares a world she will not see.

POPE PAUL VI

Youth fades; love droops, the leaves of friendship fall; A mother's secret hope outlives them all.

OLIVER WENDELL HOLMES

One generation plants the trees; another gets the shade.

CHINESE PROVERB

Bitter are the tears of a child: Sweeten them.
Deep are the thoughts of a child: Quiet them.
Sharp is the grief of a child: Take it from him.
Soft is the heart of a child: Do not harden it.

PAMELA GLENCONNER

An ounce of mother is worth a pound of clergy.

SPANISH PROVERB

Where your treasure is,
there your heart will be also.

MATTHEW 6:21 NIV

Parents can only give good advice or put them
on the right paths, but the final forming of a
person's character lies in their own hands.

ANNE FRANK

Of all the rights of women, the greatest is to be a mother.

LIN YUTANG

Your children will become what you are; so be what you want them to be.

DAVID BLY

Any woman can be a mother but it takes someone special to be called "Mom."

UNKNOWN

The greatest thing she'd learned over the years is that there's no way to be a perfect mother, but a million ways to be a good one.

UNKNOWN

*Mothers of little boys work
from son up till son down.*
UNKNOWN

*The hand that rocks the cradle
is the hand that rules the world.*
W. S. ROSS

*To the world you might be one
person, but to one person
you might be the world.*
ANONYMOUS

*As a mother, my job is to take care of what is
possible and trust God with the impossible.*
RUTH BELL GRAHAM

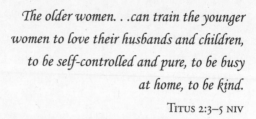

*The older women. . .can train the younger
women to love their husbands and children,
to be self-controlled and pure, to be busy
at home, to be kind.*

TITUS 2:3–5 NIV

*A mother is one to whom
you hurry when you are troubled.*

EMILY DICKINSON

The strength of motherhood
is greater than natural laws.

BARBARA KINGSOLVER

*Mama exhorted her children at every opportunity
to "jump at de sun." We might not land on the
sun, but at least we would get off the ground.*

ZORA NEALE HURSTON

"Believe in the Lord Jesus, and you will be saved—you and your household."
ACTS 16:31 NIV

Your children need your presence more than your presents.
JESSE JACKSON

Life affords no greater responsibility, no greater privilege, than the raising of the next generation.
C. EVERETT KOOP

Live so that when your children think of fairness and integrity, they think of you.
H. JACKSON BROWN

Sometimes we're so concerned about giving our children what we never had growing up, we neglect to give them what we did have growing up.

JAMES DOBSON

We cannot hope only to leave our children a bigger car, a bigger bank account. We must hope to give them a sense of what it means to be a loyal friend, a loving parent, a citizen who leaves his home, his neighborhood and town better than he found it.

GEORGE H. W. BUSH

Discipline doesn't break a child's spirit half as often as the lack of it breaks a parent's heart.

ANONYMOUS

Listen to the desires of your children.
Encourage them and then give them the
autonomy to make their own decision.
DENIS WAITLEY

Lord, through all the generations
you have been our home!
PSALM 90:1 NLT

Put the Power
in your Prayers.

Want a fresh perspective on prayer? Ready to
revitalize your prayer life?

Power Prayers for Women gives you solid
biblical reasons to pray—and specific prayer starters
for 21 key areas of life. Inside, you'll find "power
prayers" for your

- Emotions
- Home
- Fears
- Work
- Finances
- Church
- Nation
- And much more!

Quick and easy to read, yet packed with spiritual
punch, *Power Prayers for Women* is what you need
to succeed in this vital profession. Put the power in
your prayers!

Power Prayers for Women—
Revitalize Your Prayer Life
$7.97
ISBN 978-1-59789-670-2

Available wherever Christian books are sold.